Nita Mehta's
JHATPAT KHAA
Vegetarian Meals in m...

Nita Mehta's
JHATPAT KHAANA
Vegetarian Meals in minutes!

Nita Mehta

B.Sc. (Home Science), M.Sc. (Food and Nutrition), Gold Medalist

ANU KSHETRAPAL

SNAB
Publishers Pvt Ltd

Nita Mehta's **JHATPAT KHAANA** *Vegetarian Meals in minutes*

© Copyright 2000-2006 **SNAB** Publishers Pvt Ltd

WORLD RIGHTS RESERVED. The contents—all recipes, photographs and drawings are original and copyrighted. No portion of this book shall be reproduced, stored in a retrieval system or transmitted by any means, electronic, mechanical, photocopying, recording or otherwise, without the written permission of the publishers.

While every precaution is taken in the preparation of this book, the publisher and the author assume no responsibility for errors or omissions. Neither is any liability assumed for damages resulting from the use of information contained herein.

TRADEMARKS ACKNOWLEDGED. Trademarks used, if any, are acknowledged as trademarks of their respective owners. These are used as reference only and no trademark infringement is intended upon. Ajinomoto (monosodium glutamade, MSG) is a trademark of Aji-no-moto company of Japan. Use it sparingly if you must as a flavour enhancer.

6th Print 2006
ISBN 81-86004-85-8

Food Styling and Photography: **SNAB**

Layout and laser typesetting :

National Information Technology Academy
3A/3, Asaf Ali Road
New Delhi-110002
☎ 23252948

Published by :

Publishers Pvt. Ltd.
3A/3 Asaf Ali Road,
New Delhi - 110002
Tel: 23252948, 23250091
Telefax: 91-11-23250091

Editorial and Marketing office:
E-159, Greater Kailash-II, N.Delhi-48
Fax: 91-11-29225218, 29229558
Tel: 91-11-29214011, 29218727, 29218574
E-Mail: nitamehta@email.com
Website: http://www.nitamehta.com
Website: http://www.snabindia.com

Distributed by :

THE VARIETY BOOK DEPOT
A.V.G. Bhavan, M 3 Con Circus,
New Delhi - 110 001
Tel : 23417175, 23412567; Fax : 23415335
Email: varietybookdepot@rediffmail.com

Printed by :

PRESSTECH LITHO PVT LTD, NEW DELHI

Rs. 89/-

INTRODUCTION

Hard pressed for time? Jhatpat Khaana- sounds incredible but it's true. Now with this book in hand you can prepare delicious and **complete vegetarian meals in minutes** — the ones you thought would take eternity. This book is written keeping in mind the modern world of fast paced living. Women are doing double duty — taking care of the home as well as going out to work. The special chapter on meals from leftovers will be of special help for time pressed woman. Quick as well as delightful recipes are the need of the day. It may be a hearty soup with a snack or pastas served with a variety of breads. You could prepare a delicious biryani with plain curd or just a quick curry or vegetable with boiled rice, roti, bread or puri.

Jhatpat cooking is easy if you are well organized with the ingredients reqired. To make your recipes jhatpat, substitute ready made tomato puree, packed cream, ready made coconut milk, evaporated milk, canned or frozen corn and peas for fresh ones. Plan ahead and shop on weekends to stack your fridge with these. Have your family favourites like paneer, mushrooms, frozen or tinned corn, pastas, boiled potatoes etc. always handy. Rush into your kitchen, pick up available ingredients of your choice and russle up a tasty, nutritive and wholesome 'meal in minutes!'

Nita Mehta

CONTENTS

INTRODUCTION   5
STARTERS & TEA TIME SNACKS   9
    Til Paneer   10
    Cheese Pockets   13
    Nutty Spinach Slices   14
    Vegetable & Cheese Dumplings   16
    Corn Semolina Nuggets   18
    Lazeez Paneer Toasts   20
    Mushroom Dinner Rolls   22
    Bread Bhelpuri   24
    Melba Toasts   26
    Corn Kebabs   27
    Chilli Paneer Footlongs   28
SOUPS   31
    Subziyon Ka Shorba   32
    Sweet Corn Chowder   34
    Cheesy Mushroom Coriander Soup   36
    Tom Yum Soup   37

DESI DELIGHTS 41
    Jhatpat Stir Fried Paneer 42
    Til Mil Aloo Matar 44
    Jhatpat Butter Paneer 46
    Gobhi Masala 47
    KurKuri Ajwaini Bhindi 48
    Flavourful Mixed Vegetables 51
    Quick Mawa Matar 52
    Kadhai Matar 54
    Bread Dahi Bada 56
    Dudhiya Matar Khumb 58
    Achaari Baingans 60

CONTINENTAL–PASTA & BAKED DISHES 61
    Broccoli Macaroni Italiano 62
    Paneer Steak Sizzler 64
    Fettuccine Primavera 66
    Jhatpat Spinach Vegetable Bake 68
    Cauliflower & Cottage Cheese Bake 71
    Saucy Spaghetti Casserole 72

Stir Fried Veggies on a Bed of Rice   74
    Peppery Aubergines   76

RICE   78
    Daal Biryani   79
    Tahiree (Vegetable Masala Rice)   80
    Spicy Red Mexican Rice   82

MEALS OUT OF LEFTOVERS   83
    Channa Biryani   84
    Enchiladas with White Sauce   86
    Ajwaini Daal Parantha   89
    Lemon Rice   90

DESSERTS   92
    Quick Trifle   93
    Bread Pudding   94
    Creamy Lemon Dessert   96
    Quick Tiramisu   99
    Apple Crumble   102
    Kesari Seviyaan   103

STARTERS & TEA TIME SNACKS

- At a party, starters create the first impression. Why only at a party, even when our male family members - be it your son, husband or your father or brother returns tired from work after a hectic day, a jhatpat snack for him does wonders. He suddenly sounds more peppy and definitely gets into a more cheerful mood.

- The tea time snacks can be converted into starters when their size is made small by cutting them into smaller pieces and vice-versa.

TIL PANEER

Picture on facing page *Cooking time : 5 minutes*

Beautiful to look at and delicious to eat!

Serves 3-4
200 gm paneer

BATTER

4 tbsp maida
2-3 flakes garlic - crushed
1/3 cup water (approx.)
½ tsp chilli powder
½ tsp chat masala
½ tsp salt to taste

COATING

1/3 cup bread crumbs
4 tbsp til (sesame seeds), 1 tbsp sooji (semolina)
pinch of dry orange red colour, oil for frying

Vegetable & Cheese Dumplings : page 17; Til Paneer ➢

1. Cut the paneer into slices of ¼" thickness. Cut the slices diagonally to get triangles. Sprinkle salt or chat masala on both sides. Keep aside.
2. Heat oil on medium heat in a kadhai.
3. Mix all the ingredients of the batter in a shallow flat bowl.
4. Mix all the coating ingredients in large flat plate, to spread out the mixture. (See tip.)
5. Dip the paneer pieces in the batter. Remove from batter and toss in the coating mixture to coat all sides.
6. Fry the paneer pieces, one at a time, till crisp. Drain on paper napkins to absorb excess oil. Serve hot.

TiP:

⌛ The coating mixture should be spread out in a plate and not in a bowl, so that when the paneer pieces are being coated, the whole mixture does not turn soggy.

CHEESE POCKETS

Cooking time : 8 minutes *Picture on page 39*

Crisp cheesy pockets - Great combination with any soup.

Serves 4

1 thick pizza base
1/3 cup mozzarella cheese (Amul), 1/3 cup processed cheese (cheese cubes)
1 tsp oregano (dried)
1 tbsp butter, red chilli flakes or a few freshly crushed peppercorns

1. Heat oven to 200°C.
2. Cut the pizza base into half and then each half into half again to get 4 triangles. Split each triangle from the pointed end almost till the edge, leaving the edges intact, to get a pocket.
3. Mix both the cheese and oregano.
4. Fill the pockets with cheese mixture, keeping aside some for the top.
5. Place on a baking tray. Brush the triangles generously with butter.
6. Sprinkle lots of chilli flakes or crushed peppercorns. Sprinkle left over cheese. Grill for 5-6 minutes until slightly brown and crisp. Cut each piece into 3 pieces with a pizza cutter. Serve hot.

NUTTY SPINACH SLICES

Cooking time : 10 minutes

Nutty sesame seeds on toasts - A treat with saucy spaghetti casserole (p. 56.)

Serves 4-5

10-12 diagonally cut slices of a French loaf

or

6 slices of white or brown bread
2 tbsp butter
1 tsp crushed garlic

TOPPING

1 tbsp butter
4 (50 gm) mushrooms - cut into thin slices
2 cups shredded spinach (200 gm)
2 tbsp til (sesame seeds)
50 gm (2 cubes) cheese - grated
1 tsp lemon juice
salt & pepper to taste

1. Heat oven at 210°C.
2. Make garlic butter by mixing butter and garlic and apply on the bread. Grill for 7 minutes till crisp (you can also toast on a non stick tawa.)
3. Meanwhile prepare the topping. Heat 1 tbsp butter in a non stick pan or a kadhai and add mushroom slices. Saute for ½ minute and remove to a plate.
4. Heat the left over butter in the same pan. Add sesame seeds (til) and wait for 1 minute or till the seeds change colour. Add the spinach and cook till water evaporates. Add ¼ tsp each of salt and pepper. Add lemon juice and mix well. Remove from heat.
5. Spread spinach on toasted bread, spoon some mushrooms and top with grated cheese.
6. Grill for 2-3 minutes at 210°C at serving time. Cut into squares if using ordinary bread or serve whole slices if French bread slices have been used. Serve hot.

VEGETABLE & CHEESE DUMPLINGS

Picture on page 11   *Cooking time : 12 minutes*

Vegetable balls stuffed with cheese, rolled in bread crumbs and fried till golden. Sprinkle some finely grated cheese on them at the time of serving.

Serves 8

(250 gm) 2 cups roughly chopped ghiya (bottle gourd)
2 slices of bread
3/4 cup finely grated carrot (1 carrot)
3/4 cup grated cabbage
¼ cup mashed paneer (25 gm)
1 tsp salt, ½ tsp pepper, or to taste
¼ tsp each of amchoor, red chilli powder and garam masala
2 tbsp bread crumbs + some more to coat
1 cube cheese - grated (25 gm)
oil for frying

1. Pressure cook peeled and chopped ghiya with 1 tbsp water to give 1 whistle. Remove from fire and put under running water to let the pressure drop. Transfer to a plate and let it cool down.
2. Mix grated carrot, cabbage, paneer, salt, pepper, amchoor, garam masala red chilli powder and 2 tbsp bread crumbs.
3. Break the bread slices roughly and put in a blender. Grind for a few seconds to get fresh bread crumbs. Drain the steamed ghiya. Add the drained ghiya and churn to grind the ghiya along with the bread to a paste.
4. Add the ghiya paste to the carrot mixture and mix well. If the mixture feels too soft to form into balls, churn some more bread in the mixer to form crumbs and add to the ghiya mixture.
5. Make balls, flatten a little and stuff 1 tsp of grated cheese inside. Make a ball again. Roll in bread crumbs scattered in a plate.
6. Deep fry 1-2 pieces at a time, on medium heat till golden. Drain on paper napkins.
7. Arrange in a serving plate and sprinkle some finely grated cheese on them.
8. Serve with a spicy tomato ketchup as an evening snack or as a starter before the main meals.

CORN SEMOLINA NUGGETS

Cooking time : 11 minutes

Serves 4-5

½ cup suji (semolina)
1 cup milk
1 cup (150 gms) paneer (cottage cheese) - mashed
1/3 cup cooked corn kernels (fresh or tinned)
¼ cup coriander leaves - chopped
salt to taste
¼ tsp garam masala, ½ tsp red chilli flakes, ½ tsp chaat masala
2 tsp lemon juice

COATING
bread crumbs
2 tbsp maida dissolved in ¼ cup water to get a thin maida batter
oil for frying

1. Roast suji in a kadhai on low heat for 2-3 minutes. Do not let it turn pink.
2. Add milk, stirring continuously. Cook till thick. Keep on low flame for 1-2 minutes more, stirring constantly, until dry and forms a lump. Add corn and coriander. Mix well.
3. Remove from fire. Transfer to a paraat. Add all other ingredients except the coating ingredients. Mix very well. Check seasonings.
4. Make small heart shaped cutlets. Dip them in maida batter. Roll in bread crumbs spread on a plate.
5. Deep fry 2-3 pieces at a time.

TiP: To make crisper nuggets keep them in the fridge, for 15-20 minutes before frying, to set them well.

LAZEEZ PANEER TOASTS

Cooking time : 11 minutes

All time favourite!

Serves 4

1½ tbsp butter
4 slices brown or white bread
1 tsp garlic (5-6 flakes) - crushed and chopped
100 gm (25-30) leaves of paalak (spinach) - washed & shredded
150 gm paneer (cottage cheese)
1 tbsp basil or coriander - chopped
5 tbsp mozzarella cheese (Amul) - grated
¼ tsp salt and pepper, or to taste
some red chilli flakes

1. Wash and shred the spinach leaves into thin ribbons. Pat dry on a kitchen towel.
2. Heat butter in a kadhai or pan.
3. Add garlic and stir. Add the spinach and cook till all the moisture of the spinach evaporates. Remove from heat.
4. Mean while grate the paneer in a bowl. Add basil or coriander and 4 tbsp grated mozzarella cheese, leaving behind 1 tbsp for the topping.
5. Add cooked spinach to the paneer and mix well. Add salt and pepper.
6. Toast the slices and spread the mixture on the toasts. Sprinkle some mozzarella cheese. Sprinkle some red chilli flakes too.
7. Grill in the oven (210°C) for 2-3 minutes and serve hot cut into triangles or squares.

Jhatpat TiP:

- Preheat the oven before preparing the mixture.
- Toast the slices while preparing the mixture.

MUSHROOM DINNER ROLLS

Cooking time : 9 minutes

It makes a complete meal with a baked dish or pasta.

Serves 6-8

6-8 small dinner rolls (small buns) or 4 small hot dog buns
1-2 tbsp melted butter

FILLING

100 gm mushrooms - cut into small thin slices
1½ tbsp butter, 1 tbsp maida
3/4 cup milk
1 green chilli - chopped or ½ capsicum - chopped
2 tbsp chopped coriander, salt & pepper to taste

TOPPING

25 gm (1 cube) cheese - grated
red chilli flakes and prepared English mustard

1. Heat oven to 210°C.
2. Cut a thin slice from the top of the dinner roll and with the back of a spoon, scoop out the centre, leaving a thick shell all around, to get a small hollow. Brush the scooped hollow and the out sides with melted butter. Place on a grill tray. Grill for 5 minutes at 210°C or till crisp.
3. Meanwhile prepare the filling: heat ½ tbsp butter in a kadhai or non stick pan and add the mushrooms and saute for 1 minute. Remove on to a plate. In the same sauce pan add 1 tbsp of butter and add the flour. Cook till slightly brown, lower heat and add the milk. Cook till quite thick. Add the mushrooms, green chilli or capsicum, coriander or parsley, salt & pepper to taste. Remove from heat.
4. Remove the crisp buns from the oven and spoon some filling in hollow or scooped portion.
5. Sprinkle cheese and return to the oven for 2 minutes or till cheese melts. Sprinkle chilli flakes and dot with mustard. Serve with a hearty soup to make up a complete meal.

Jhatpat TiP:
- Grill the empty hollow buns while preparing the filling.
- You can use finely chopped broccoli also instead of mushrooms.

BREAD BHELPURI

Cooking time : 6 minutes

Spicy and delicious!

Serves 4

3 slices bread
chaat masala to taste, salt to taste
1 onion - chopped finely
2 green chillies - chopped finely, 1 tbsp chopped coriander
1 cup (50 gms) namkeen sev (Bikaneri bhujiya)
1 cup fresh annar ke dane (pomegranate seeds) or 1 tomato - chopped finely
2 tbsp khatti mithi chutney (given below), 2 tbsp poodina (mint) ki chutney
oil for frying, lemon rings to serve

QUICK KHATTI MITHI CHUTNEY
(cook all together till thick)

1 tbsp amchoor (dried mango powder), 3 tbsp sugar or shakkar (gur)
½ tsp bhuna jeera (roasted cumin seeds) powder
¼ tsp red chilli powder, ¼ tsp salt, ¼ tsp garam masala
¼ cup water

1. Mix all ingredients of the khatti mithi chutney together in a small heavy bottomed pan. Cook on low flame, till all the ingredients dissolve properly and the chutney reaches the right consistency. Keep aside to cool.
2. Cut bread slices into (¼") tiny square pieces. Deep fry to a golden brown colour.
3. Mix onion, annar, sev, green chillies and chopped coriander.
4. Sprinkle some chaat masala.
5. Add chutneys to taste. Mix well.
6. Add fried bread cubes in the end just before serving otherwise the bhel turns soggy.
7. Arrange one or two cabbage leaves in a bowl. Fill with the prepared bhelpuri and sprinkle some more sev and annar on top.
8. Serve immediately, garnished with lemon rings otherwise it tends to get soggy.

MELBA TOASTS

Cooking time : 8 minutes

A very light starter which will be relished with any soup.

Serves 4

4 slices of a day old bread
3 tbsp butter
1½ tsp garlic paste (8-10 flakes - crushed)
¼ tsp pepper
lemon rind of 1 lemon (grate a whole lemon very lightly)
1 tsp lemon juice
1 tbsp finely chopped fresh parsley, basil or coriander

1. Heat oven to 200°C.
2. Trim the edges of the bread slices.
3. In a bowl mix together - butter, garlic, lemon rind, parsley/coriander/basil, lemon juice and pepper.
4. Spread the flavoured butter on one side of the slice.
5. Grill in a hot oven for 7 minutes or till crisp. Cut the slice in 2 triangles. Serve with a soup.

CORN KEBABS

Cooking time : 7 minutes **Picture on cover**

Crisp and crunchy!

Serves 4

2 tender, large fresh bhuttas - grated (1 cup) or 1 cup tinned or frozen corn, blended coarsely in a grinder, 2 slices bread
1" piece ginger - grated, 1 green chilli - chopped finely
2 tbsp coriander or mint - chopped finely, a few tbsp milk to bind, optional
½ tsp garam masala, ½ tsp amchoor, salt to taste, 2-3 tbsp oil for frying
hari chutney and tomato ketchup to garnish

1. Break the bread slices roughly and grind in a mixer for a few seconds to get crumbled bread. Add crumbled bread to the grated corn.
2. Add chopped coriander or mint, ginger, green chillies, garam masala, amchoor and salt. Mix well. If the mixture feels too dry, add 3-4 tbsp milk to bind the mixture. Shape the mixture into small, round, flattened kebabs.
3. Heat a non stick pan with a little oil. Shallow fry on both sides till golden.
4. Serve dotted with a blob of hari chutney and a dot of tomato ketchup on the hari chutney.

CHILLI PANEER FOOTLONGS

Picture on facing page　　　　　　　　　　　　*Cooking time : 17 minutes*

The perfect snack for the ever hungry growing children.

Serves 8

1 loaf long French bread or garlic bread, some butter to spread
100 gm pizza cheese - grated
1 spring onion - chopped along with greens or ¼ capsicum and ¼ onion - diced
2½ tbsp maida (plain flour), some crushed peppercorns and red chilli flakes

TOMATO SPREAD

6-8 flakes garlic - crushed
¼ tsp red chilli paste or powder
½ cup ready made tomato puree, 2 tbsp tomato sauce
1 tsp oregano (dried) or ½ tsp ajwain
salt and pepper to taste
1-2 tbsp oil

CHILLI PANEER

100 gms paneer - cut into ¼" cubes
½ tbsp soya sauce

½ tbsp vinegar
¼ tsp salt and ¼ tsp pepper
½ tsp red chilli paste or red chilli powder
½ tsp garlic paste (3-4 garlic flakes - crushed)

1. Marinate paneer with soya sauce, vinegar, salt, pepper, chilli paste and crushed garlic.
2. Sprinkle maida on the paneer. Mix gently to coat. Deep fry in 2 batches till golden brown.
3. To prepare the spread, heat oil. Add garlic and cook till light brown. Add all the other ingredients and cook on low flame till thick. Keep aside.
4. To assemble, cut the loaf into two lengthwise. Butter each piece on the cut surface and the sides too.
5. Spread some tomato spread, sprinkle some grated cheese and then arrange the fried chilli paneer. Press.
6. Top with some spring onions or diced capsicum and onions. Spread some more cheese. Sprinkle some crushed peppercorns and red chilli flakes. Keep aside till serving time.
7. To serve, grill at 180°C for 8-10 minutes or till cheese melts. Cut into 4 pieces and serve.

SOUPS

With so many ready made soups available in the market, one gets tempted to avoid preparing a fresh soup. Remember, these ready made soups can never give the same nutritional benefits as the fresh ones. Besides, sometimes they may even be a little unhealthy since most of them contain the taste enhancer - Monosodium Glutamate (ajinomoto).

Here are some pressure cooked jhatpat soup recipes. Generally, in soup making, the vegetables are pureed after cooking. Hence there is a long wait till the vegetables cool down before they are ready to be churned in the mixer to get the pureed soup. In the following soups, the ingredients are pureed in the mixer before they are cooked, so there is no cooling time required to blend in a mixer. They can be served straight off the stove. Give them a try and you will never regret not using a ready made packet!

SUBZIYON KA SHORBA

Cooking time : 11 minutes

Mixed vegetables in a tomato based shorba, tempered with cumin.

Serves 4

500 gm tomatoes - chopped roughly
1 potato - peeled and chopped roughly
3-4 flakes garlic - crushed or chopped
1" piece ginger - chopped
1 green chilli - chopped
10-12 leaves of poodina (mint)
¼ tsp red chilli powder
1 tsp salt & ½ tsp sugar, or to taste

TEMPERING
1 tbsp butter or oil, 1 tsp jeera (cumin seeds)
mixed vegetables - 1 small floret cauliflower, ½ carrot, 1" piece of cabbage &
1-2 French beans

1. In a pressure cooker add tomatoes, potato, garlic, ginger, green chilli and mint.
2. Add salt, sugar and chilli powder. Add 4 cups of water. Close the lid and pressure cook to give 2 whistles. Reduce heat and cook for ½ minute.
3. Meanwhile chop the beans into very tiny pieces and grate the cabbage, cauliflower and carrot coarsely. If you wish cut all the vegetables very finely instead of grating them. The mixed vegetables should be about 1 cup.
4. Remove the pressure cooker from heat. Drop the pressure by putting the cooker under water.
5. Open the lid and strain the soup through a soup strainer, pressing with a metal spoon or ladle (karchhi) to get all the extract. Discard the residue. Keep the shorba aside.
6. Heat butter or oil in a clean pan. Add jeera. Wait till it turns golden. Add the vegetables and stir fry for 1 minute.
7. Add the strained shorba and bring to a boil. Cook covered till the vegetables turn slightly tender. Adjust the seasonings.
8. Garnish with chopped mint and serve hot in soup bowls with a spoon.

SWEET CORN CHOWDER

Cooking time: 7 minutes

A filling soup for the family. Serve in soup bowls with a spoon to relish the corn niblets. Enjoy a light snack such as melba toasts (p. 26) with this hearty soup.

Serves 4

2 tbsp butter
½ cup tinned corn nibblets
8-10 leaves paalak (spinach) - shredded finely
1 small tomato - deseeded and chopped (¼ cup)
1 small onion - chopped finely
¼ cup finely chopped carrot (½ of a small carrot)
¼ cup finely chopped potato (½ of a potato)
1 tbsp cornflour dissolved in ¼ cup milk
1 tsp salt and ½ tsp pepper, or to taste
a pinch of sugar
1 tbsp chopped coriander or parsley

1. Peel and cut potato and carrot lengthwise into ¼" thick slices. Cut the slices into tiny pieces (dice). Chop onions and tomato finely.
2. Heat butter in a sauce pan. Add onion, carrot and potatoes. Stir fry ½ minute.
3. Add corn, spinach, salt, pepper and a pinch of sugar. Stir.
4. Add the tomatoes and 4 cups of water. Boil. Reduce heat. Cover and simmer for 2 minutes.
5. Add cornflour dissolved in milk and stir. Give 1 boil. Add coriander or parsley. Remove from fire.

TiP:

- If you use fresh corn, boil whole corn in water with a little salt, sugar and a pinch of haldi for colour. Boil for 5 minutes and do not over cook, as corn toughens on overcooking. Cool. Grind coarsely and use.

CHEESY MUSHROOM CORIANDER SOUP

Cooking time : 8 minutes

Serves 8

200 gm mushrooms - chopped into very thin, small pieces
½ tbsp butter, 1 large onion - sliced thinly, ½" piece ginger - grated finely
2 tea cups of milk (cold) mixed with 3 tbsp corn flour
2 tsp salt, or to taste & white pepper to taste, 2-3 tbsp chopped coriander
juice of ½ lemon, 1 cube (20 gm) grated cheese - to garnish

1. Heat ½ tbsp butter in a pressure cooker. Add onion and ginger & stir well.
2. Add the mushrooms and stir for 2-3 minutes.
3. Add 6 cups of water and close the lid of the pressure cooker and pressure cook to give 1-2 whistles. Simmer on low heat for ½ minute. Remove from heat. Drop pressure by putting the cooker under water. Open the lid.
4. Return the pressure cooker to heat without the lid. Dissolve cornflour in cold milk and add to the soup. Add salt, pepper and coriander. Boil. Simmer for 1 minute.
5. Remove from fire and mix in the lemon juice. Stir gently to mix. Serve hot garnished with grated cheese.

TOM YUM SOUP

Cooking time : 10 minutes **Picture on page 39**

A clear, hot and sour Thai soup.

Serves 4

STOCK

6 cups water
1" piece ginger - finely chopped
¼ tsp hing (asafoetida), 10 saboot kaali mirch (peppercorns)
very thinly grated rind of 1 lemon or 2 stalks lemon grass, 1½ tsp salt
2 dry, red chillies, 1 cup chopped cabbage, 1 potato - chopped

OTHER INGREDIENTS

2 tbsp oil
2-3 baby corns-cut into paper thin slices, 3 mushrooms-cut into paper thin slices
½ carrot - cut into paper thin diagonal slices, 4 spinach leaves, tear into half
¼ tsp red chilli powder
juice of 1½" piece ginger, juice of 1 lemon
salt and pepper to taste
2 tsp (level) cornflour mixed with 2 tbsp water

1. To prepare the stock, pressure cook all the ingredients together. After the first whistle, keep on low heat for 6-7 minutes.
2. While stock is on fire, cut vegetables into really thin slices. (See tip.)
3. Wash and grate 1½" piece of ginger along with the peel. Squeeze the grated ginger with your hands or through a muslin cloth to get juice.
4. Heat oil in a pan. Add baby corns, mushrooms and carrots. Saute for 2 minutes on medium flame. Reduce heat. Add red chilli powder and stir for 2-3 seconds. Add the spinach leaves. Remove from fire.
5. Strain the stock into the vegetables. Return to fire. Add cornflour paste.
6. Squeeze lemon juice and ginger juice into the clear soup. Add salt and pepper to taste. Boil. Simmer for 2 minutes. Serve hot in soup bowls.

TiP:

- Cut vegetables into really thin slices so that they float on the soup when served. If thick, they will sink to the bottom, since it is a clear soup and is not thick.

- While taking out the lemon rind, grate the whole lemon very lightly on the grater without applying any pressure. If the lemon is not grated carefully,

Cheese Pockets : recipe on page 13; Tom Yum Soup : recipe on page 37 ➤

the white portion (pith) beneath the lemon peel also comes along with the rind. The pith imparts a bitter taste to the soup.

- The best option is to use a stalk of fresh lemon grass in the stock, but since it is not easily available, lemon rind may be substituted. You may substitute dry lemon grass also if fresh stalks are not available.

DESI DELIGHTS

Indian curries don't need long hours in the kitchen any longer. Short cuts are given, without affecting the end results. Stir fried vegetables which take just a few minutes to cook are also included. Stir fried vegetables cooked and served immediately always taste better than those which are cooked hours before serving time and reheated several times. They lose their natural colour & crispness.

To make Jhatpat vegetables, a few things should be kept in mind. If cutting large pieces or florets of broccoli or cauliflower, cut them into flat, thin pieces. Vegetables cut in a small, uniform size and shape cook faster and better.

JHATPAT STIR FRIED PANEER

Cooking time : 5 minutes

Serves 4

200 gm paneer - cut into fingers
3 tbsp oil
½ tsp jeera
2 dried, red chillies - broken into pieces & deseeded
1 onion - sliced thinly
1 capsicum - deseeded & cut into thin fingers
1 tomato - cut into four lengthways, remove pulp and cut into thin long pieces
2 tbsp tomato puree
¼ tsp dhania powder (coriander), ¼ tsp red chilli powder, ¼ tsp garam masala
1 tsp salt, or to taste
1 tbsp chopped green coriander
1" piece ginger - shredded or cut into match sticks

1. Slice onion, capsicum and tomato lengthwise.
2. Heat oil in a kadhai.
3. Reduce heat. Add jeera and red chillies. Let jeera turn golden.
4. Add onion and stir fry for a minute till slightly cooked.
5. Add the capsicum and stir for ½ minute.
6. Add dhania powder, red chillies, garam masala and ½ tsp salt.
7. Add the paneer and tomato puree and stir till the paneer is well coated. Add ½ tsp salt on the paneer.
8. Add tomato slices, coriander and shredded ginger (or ginger match sticks). Mix and remove from heat. Serve hot.

TiP:

- You may substitute shredded cabbage instead of capsicum.

TIL MIL ALOO MATAR

Cooking time : 8 minutes

Serves 4

4 small sized potatoes - boiled
1½ tbsp til (sesame seeds)
3/4 tsp jeera (cumin seeds)
3 tbsp oil
1 large onion - chopped very finely
4-5 cashew - split into halves
10-15 kishmish - soaked in water
3/4 cup boiled or frozen peas
1 tsp salt, or to taste
¼ tsp haldi
½ tsp garam masala, ½ tsp red chilli powder, ½ tsp amchoor
2-3 tbsp chopped coriander
2 green chillies - slit lengthwise

1. Boil potatoes in salted water until just tender. They should feel soft when a knife is inserted. Do not over cook. (You may also microwave the potatoes if you wish, 4 potatoes would take about 4 minutes on full power, or pressure cook the potatoes for a quicker subzi).
2. Peel and cut each potato widthwise into 2 equal halves.
3. Heat oil. Add til and jeera. Wait till the til (sesame seeds) start changing colour.
4. Add onions. Cook until onions turn light brown.
5. Add kaju. Stir-fry for a minute. Add kishmish.
6. Add salt, haldi, garam masala, red chilli powder and amchoor. Mix.
7. Add green chillies and fresh coriander. Cook for 1 minute.
8. Add 2-3 tbsp water.
9. Add the potatoes. Stir-fry gently for about 3 minutes on low heat, taking care not to break the potatoes.
10. Finally, add peas. Mix gently. Cook for 2 minutes stirring occasionally. Remove from fire. Serve hot.

JHATPAT BUTTER PANEER

Cooking time : 7 minutes

Serves 4

150 gm paneer - cut into ¼" thick and 1" square pieces
200 gm (3) tomatoes - blended to a smooth puree, 3 tbsp tomato puree
2 tbsp oil, 1 tbsp butter, ¼ tsp shah jeera
2 tbsp broken cashewnuts - soaked in some water
¼ tsp chilli powder, ¼ tsp garam masala, 1 tsp salt, or to taste
¼-½ tsp sugar, 1 tsp kasoori methi
¼ cup milk, ½ cup water

1. Heat oil and butter. Add shah jeera. Wait for 30 seconds. Add the freshly pureed tomatoes and cook till the juices of the tomatoes evaporates and masala gets dry. Add tomato puree.
2. Meanwhile grind cashews to a smooth paste with some water.
3. To the tomato masala, add cashewnut paste, chilli powder, garam masala and salt. Stir. Reduce heat. Add milk. Stir. Add water and kasoori methi.
4. Add paneer. Add sugar (depending on the sourness of tomatoes.) Simmer for 1-2 minutes. Serve garnished with coriander & slit green chillies.

GOBHI MASALA

Picture on page 49 *Cooking time : 9 minutes*

Serves 4

1 medium cauliflower - broken into medium florets
2 tbsp oil, ½ tsp jeera, 1" piece ginger - grated
4 tbsp tomato puree
1 tbsp kasoori methi, 2 tsp tomato ketchup
½ tsp garam masala, 1½ tsp dhania powder, 3/4 tsp salt, or to taste
½ tsp red chilli powder
a few ginger match sticks, chopped coriander and slit green chillies to garnish

1. Deep fry cauliflower in 2 batches till golden brown. Drain on paper napkins.
2. Heat 2 tbsp oil. Add jeera. When golden, add ginger. Stir for a minute.
3. Add tomato puree. Mix well. Reduce heat. Add garam masala, dhania powder, salt, and red chilli powder. Cook for 2 minutes.
4. Add kasoori methi and tomato ketchup.
5. Add ¼ cup water. Boil. Simmer on low heat for 1 minute. Reduce heat.
6. Add the fried cauliflower to the masala. Mix well and garnish with slit green chillies, chopped coriander and ginger match sticks.

KURKURI AJWAINI BHINDI

Picture on facing page *Cooking time : 10 minutes*

Serves 2-3

250 gm bhindi (lady fingers)
3 tbsp besan (gram flour)
½ tsp ajwain (carom seeds)
¼ tsp haldi
2 tsp chaat masala
1 tsp chilli powder
juice of ½ lemon (1 tbsp)
½ tsp salt, or to taste
oil for frying

Gobhi Masala : recipe on page 47; Kurkuri Ajwaini Bhindi ➢

1. Wash and pat dry bhindi. Cut the head and slit the bhindi into four lengthwise. Place in a shallow bowl or paraat.
2. Heat oil in a kadhai for frying.
3. Sprinkle ajwain, haldi, chaat masala, dry besan and salt on the bhindi.
4. Sprinkle lemon juice and toss well to coat the bhindi.
5. Add half of the bhindi to hot oil and fry in 2 batches till crisp. Drain on absorbent paper. Serve hot with khitchri or dal chawal.

TiP:

- Mix all the ingredients to the bhindi at the time of frying as the salt added releases moisture which can make the bhindi soggy.

- To make it really jhatpat, put the oil on fire to get hot. In the meanwhile cut half of the bhindi first and sprinkle all the other ingredients and fry the first batch. While the first batch is being fried, cut the left over bhindi.

FLAVOURFUL MIXED VEGETABLES

Cooking time : 7 minutes *Picture on cover*

Serves 4

2 capsicums - cut into 8-12 pieces (1" cubes)
2 boiled potatoes - cut into 8 pieces (1" cubes)
2 carrots - peeled and cut into ½" thick, round slices
2 tomatoes - cut into 8 pieces (1" cubes)
juice of 1 lemon, 3 tbsp oil, ½ tsp jeera, 1" piece ginger - chopped, ¼ tsp haldi

FLAVOURFUL MASALA

seeds of 2 chhoti illaichi (green cardamoms), seeds of 2 moti illaichi (black cardamom), 2 laung (cloves), 1" stick dalchini (cinnamon)

1. Boil 1 cup water with ½ tsp salt. Add the cubed carrots. Cover and cook till just done. Do not over cook. Strain and keep aside.
2. Meanwhile, crush all ingredients of the flavourful masala to a rough powder.
3. Heat oil in a kadhai. Add jeera. Let it turn golden. Add ginger. Add haldi. Add potatoes and bhuno for 2-3 minutes.
4. Add capsicum, carrots & tomatoes together. Add 1 tsp salt (or to taste) & 1 tsp flavourful masala. Stir fry for 2 minutes. Squeeze lemon juice. Serve.

QUICK MAWA MATAR

Cooking time : 8 minutes

Serves 4

2½ cups fresh or frozen peas - boiled in water till soft
½ cup skimmed milk powder - dissolved in ½ cup water
3 tbsp oil
1 tsp jeera (cumin seeds)
2 green chillies - deseeded & finely chopped
1" piece ginger - finely chopped
4 tbsp ready made tomato puree
3/4 tsp garam masala
1 tsp salt, or to taste
3/4 tsp red chilli powder
3/4 tsp amchoor
2 tbsp coriander - chopped fresh

1. Heat oil in a kadhai. Add jeera.
2. When jeera turns golden, add ginger and green chillies. Stir till ginger turns light brown.
3. Add tomato puree. Bhuno for 1 minute.
4. Add garam masala, salt, chilli powder and amchoor.
5. Add peas. Mix well.
6. Add the milk powder paste and cook on medium flame for 4-5 minutes or until the masala thickens, stirring gently.
7. Serve hot with chappaties, garnished with fresh coriander.

KADHAI MATAR

Cooking time : 8 minutes

Serves 4

A chilli hot and colourful dish.
2 cups shelled peas
3 tbsp oil
¼ tsp methi daana (fenugreek seeds), 1-2 whole, dry red chillies
1 tbsp ginger-garlic paste
3/4 tsp garam masala, ½ tsp red chilli powder, 1 tsp dhania powder
1 tsp lemon juice
3 tomatoes - chopped finely
3/4 tsp salt or to taste
¼ tsp sugar
seeds of 1 moti illaichi (black cardamom) - powdered
1 tbsp kasoori methi (dry fenugreek leaves)
1 green chilli - deseeded & slit lengthwise
2 tbsp fresh coriander - chopped

1. Heat 3 tbsp oil in a kadhai, add methi daana and whole red chillies. Let methi dana turn golden.
2. Add ginger-garlic paste and saute over medium heat for ½ minute.
3. Add garam masala, red chilli powder, dhania powder.
4. Add lemon juice and tomatoes and saute for 5-7 minutes until the tomatoes get well blended.
5. Add the shelled green peas and mix well. Add sugar & salt.
6. Add crushed seeds of 1 moti illaichi, kasoori methi, green chillies and green coriander. Stir fry for 1 minute.
7. Serve hot with paranthas or roti.

BREAD DAHI BADA

Cooking time : 10 minutes

Serves 4

8 slices of bread
½ tsp jeera to top
8 kishmish (raisins) - washed and soaked in water
2 cups dahi - whipped & spiced with bhuna jeera, kala namak and other spices

FILLING

3 tsp very finely cut ginger, 2 tbsp finely chopped coriander
6-8 almonds - chopped very finely
¼ tsp salt, ¼ tsp red chilli, ¼ tsp garam masala
2 green chillies - deseeded and chopped very finely
oil for frying

BATTER

¼ cup maida, ½ cup water
a pinch of haldi, ¼ tsp salt, ¼ tsp red chilli powder

QUICK KHATTI MITHI CHUTNEY (P. 24)

1. Prepare a thin bater by mixing all ingredients of the batter together.
2. Mix all ingredients of the filling together - ginger, coriander, almonds, green chillies, salt, garam masala and red chilli powder. Keep aside.
3. Heat oil for deep frying.
4. Cut two rounds with a biscuit cutter or a kulfi mould's cap from each slice of bread.
5. Put some filling on a round piece of bread. Place 1 kishmish on top. Cover with another round and press the two together to join the two pieces of bread. Make 8 such pieces.
6. When the oil is well heated, dip each piece in batter. Press some jeera (cumin seeds) on it and put it in hot oil for frying. The bada swells in oil.
7. Fry one piece at a time. Drain on paper napkins.
8. Beat dahi with ½ tsp bhuna jeera, ¼ tsp kala namak, salt and red chilli powder to taste.
9. Dip the badas in spiced dahi and arrange in a serving dish. Pour the rest of the dahi on top. Sprinkle some bhuna jeera and red chilli powder.
10. Keep in the fridge to let the bread badas get soaked in the dahi for about ½ hour. Serve cold with quick khatti mithi chutney given on page 24.

DUDHIYA MATAR KHUMB

Picture on backcover **Cooking time : 15 minutes**

Serves 4-5

1½ cups shelled, boiled peas (fresh or frozen)
100 gm mushrooms - washed well and each cut into four pieces
½" stick dalchini (cinnamon)
2 moti illaichi (black cardamoms)
3-4 laung (cloves)
2 tbsp cashewnuts - soaked and ground to a smooth paste
4 tbsp oil
2 onions - ground to a paste
2 green chillies - chopped
1 tsp dhania powder
1 tbsp ginger garlic paste (1" piece ginger & 5-6 flakes garlic)
1 cup dahi mixed with 1 tsp cornflour - beat very well till very smooth
¼ cup water
3 tbsp kasoori methi (dry fenugreek leaves)
1½ tsp salt, or to taste, ¼ tsp sugar, depending on the sourness of curd
3/4 cup milk (approx.)

1. Boil peas in salted water till tender.
2. Crush together dalchini, laung and seeds of moti illaichi to a rough powder.
3. Grind cashewnuts separately to paste with some water.
4. Heat oil. Add grated onion and green chillies. Cook on low heat till oil separates. Do not let the onions turn brown.
5. In the meanwhile heat 1 tbsp oil in a clean kadhai and stir fry the mushrooms till they turn light brown and all the water evaporates. Remove from kadhai when done.
6. To the onion masala, add ginger-garlic paste and dhania powder. Mix.
7. Add the freshly ground masala. Cook for 1-2 minutes.
8. Remove from heat. Wait for a minute for the masala to cool down. Add whisked curd.
9. Return to heat and add ¼ cup water immediately. Boil on low heat.
10. Add the kasoori methi and salt.
11. Add cashewnut paste and cook for a few seconds.
12. Add enough milk (3/4 cup) to get a thick gravy. Add the mushrooms.
13. Boil the gravy. Simmer covered on low heat for 5 minutes.
14. Add the boiled peas and a pinch of sugar. Stir for a few seconds. Serve hot.

ACHAARI BAINGANS

Cooking time : 17 minutes

Serves 4

400 gm chhote baingan (brinjals), 3 tbsp oil

ACHAARI MASALA

1 tbsp oil, 5-6 flakes garlic - crushed to a paste
1" piece ginger - chopped and crushed to a paste, 1 onion - grated
1 tsp saunf (fennel), 1 tsp rai powder (brown mustard seeds)
½ tsp each of garam masala, haldi & red chilli powder
1 tsp dhania powder, 1 tsp amchoor powder, 1½ tsp salt

1. Wash baingans and give two cuts crossing each other, more than half way, almost till the end, keeping the end intact. Keep aside.
2. Mix all ingredients of the achaari masala.
3. Fill the brinjals nicely with the masala, pushing it down with a knife.
4. Heat 3 tbsp oil in a big, heavy bottomed kadhai. Add baingans. Stir to mix well. Cover and cook, spreading them in the kadhai and stirring occasionally, for 15 minutes or till done. Do not stir frequently, otherwise they might break. Serve hot.

CONTINENTAL
PASTA AND BAKED DISHES

When you wish for a change, a bowl of cheesy pasta or some vegetables in a truly delicious continental sauce is very satisfying. Try out these quick and easy recipes, guaranteed to satisfy the most demanding appetites.

- ⌛ Pasta absorbs lots of water so use a big pan with lots of water for boiling the pasta. Bring water to a boil before adding pasta.
- ⌛ Stir pasta every 2 minutes so that it does not stick to the bottom of the pan. Boil 50-75 gm of pasta per person.
- ⌛ Pasta tends to absorb moisture so it should be put in the sauce only at the time of serving.
- ⌛ Boil pasta in plenty of water for about 7-8 minutes till al dente - tender, but resistance to bite. If over-cooked, the pasta turns mushy and loses it's shape. After removing the pasta from fire, strain and refresh in cold water. Strain and coat it with a few tsp of olive oil or cooking oil. At serving time put the pasta into hot sauce or pour hot sauce over warm pasta placed in a serving dish.

BROCCOLI MACARONI ITALIANO

Picture on page 1 *Cooking time : 9 minutes*

Serves 2-3

1 cup uncooked macaroni

SAUCE

3 tbsp olive oil or 2 tbsp butter
1 tbsp garlic - crushed
1 medium head (150-200 gm) broccoli - cut into medium florets
4-5 (50 gm) baby corns - cut into ¼" thick round slices (½ cup)
3 tomatoes - chopped very finely
2 tbsp tomato puree, 1 tbsp tomato ketchup
¼ cup thin cream or milk
½ tsp each of oregano & red chilli flakes, 1 tsp salt, or to taste
50 gm cheese, preferably mozzarella cheese

1. Boil 5 cups of water with 1 tsp salt and 1 tsp oil. Add macaroni to boiling water. Boil for 5 minutes or till almost done. Leave in hot water for a 2-3 minutes to get completely done. Strain and refresh in cold water.

2. While the macaroni is boiling, crush and chop garlic, cut broccoli into florets and baby corn into small round pieces. Keep aside.
3. Heat oil or butter in a kadhai or a non stick pan, add garlic, stir.
4. Add the broccoli. Stir for a minute. Cover on low heat for 2-3 minutes till tender, but firm.
5. Add baby corns and stir for 2 minutes.
6. Add tomatoes and cook till tomatoes turn soft.
7. Add tomato puree, tomato ketchup, oregano, chill flakes and salt. Mix.
8. Add macaroni. Stir gently till macaroni is well coated.
9. Add cream or milk. Pour into a serving dish & garnish with grated cheese.

TiP:

- As macaroni absorbs moisture, the sauce should be slightly thin to coat the macaroni well. The macaroni should only be added at the time of serving.

- You may use paneer instead of baby corns. Cut paneer into small pieces and add at step 8 along with the boiled macaroni.

PANEER STEAK SIZZLER

Cooking time : 12 minutes

Serves 2

200 gm paneer (only 100 gm is used)
1 tbsp oil
½ tsp freshly ground pepper and salt to taste

SIZZLER SAUCE

1 tbsp oil, 1 tsp garlic - crushed
2-3 mushrooms - thinly sliced
2 tbsp tomato puree, 2 tbsp tomato sauce
1 tsp worcestershire sauce
1 tsp cornflour - dissolved in 3/4 cup water
½ tsp red chilli flakes, ¼ tsp salt, or to taste

VEGETABLES

1 floret cauliflower - cut into 2-3 flat pieces
1 carrot - cut into thin diagonal slices
6-8 beans - threaded and cut into 1" long pieces
1 tbsp butter

1. Cut the paneer into ½" thick slices. Cut round pieces from the slices with a biscuit cuter or a small katori, to get 2 paneer steaks.
2. Make criss cross incisions (not too deep cuts) on both sides of the paneer steak. Marinate with salt & pepper and keep aside.
3. To prepare the sauce, heat 1 tbsp oil. Reduce heat and add garlic. Stir and then add the mushrooms. Reduce heat.
4. Mix together in a cup - tomato puree, tomato sauce and worcestershire sauce. Add to the mushrooms. Add salt and chilli flakes. Stir and add the cornflour mixture also. Cook till the sauce turns thick. Keep aside.
6. Blanch the vegetables in boiling water or microwave on high power for 3 minutes. Saute the vegetables in 1 tbsp of butter.
7. Heat 1 tbsp oil on a non stick tawa and cook paneer on low heat till crisp & brown on both sides. Do not cook on high heat as it will turn hard.
8. Heat the sizzler plate by placing directly on fire. When hot, reduce heat. Place 2 cabbage leaves. On the leaves, place the paneer steak. Arrange the vegetables on the side. Pour the hot sauce over the paneer and vegetables and also on the empty portions of the iron plate for the sauce to sizzle. Drop dots of butter here & there. Pick the hot iron plate with a pair of tongs (sansi or pakad) and place on the wooden stand. Serve.

FETTUCCINE PRIMAVERA

Cooking time : 8 minutes

Flat ribbon pasta in a cream based cheese sauce.

Serves 2-3

100 gm Fettuccine (flat ribbon pasta) - boiled (2-2½ cups)
3 tbsp olive oil or 2 tbsp butter
3-4 flakes garlic - crushed
75 gm mushrooms - cut into thin slices
2 spring onions - cut diagonally into slices
1 red or green or yellow capsicum - cut into four and then cut widthwise into thin pieces
5-6 baby corns - cut into diagonal slices of about ¼" thickness
½ cup cream
½ cup grated cheese, preferably mozzarella
¼ tsp pepper
¼ tsp red chilli flakes
salt to taste

1. Boil 4 cups of water with 1 tsp salt. When the water starts to boil, gradually slide in the fettuccine from the side of the pan. Stir well. Boil for about 4-5 minutes till done.
2. While the fettuccine is boiling, heat olive oil or butter in a pan or kadhai.
3. Add garlic. Stir for a few seconds. Add mushroom slices. Cook for 1-2 minutes on high flame.
4. Add spring onions, baby corns and capsicum and stir fry for 1 minute.
5. Add salt, pepper and chilli flakes.
6. Reduce heat and add the cream. Bring to a boil on low heat.
7. Add cheese, leaving aside some for the top. Mix well till smooth. Remove from fire. Keep sauce aside.
8. Drain the fettuccine and refresh under cold water. Add to the hot sauce and stir well to coat nicely in cream sauce.
9. Serve immediately, sprinkled with some cheese. If you want to serve later, always remember to cover when heating the pasta as the edges of the pasta tend to turn hard if not covered.

JHATPAT SPINACH VEGETABLE BAKE

Picture on facing page   *Cooking time : 15 minutes*

Serves 4

350 gm (½ bundle) paalak (spinach)
1 tsp garlic (6-7 flakes) - crushed & chopped, 1-2 green chillies - chopped
1 tbsp butter
salt & pepper to taste
2½ cups milk
1½ tbsp cornflour, 1 tbsp maida
1 tej patta (bay leaf), 1" stick dalchini (cinnamon)
2 cups finely chopped mixed vegetables (½ carrot, ¼ of a cauliflower, ¼ cup shelled peas, 5-6 beans)
4 tbsp mozzarella or pizza cheese - grated, 1 tbsp butter
1 tsp salt, ½ tsp pepper and ¼ tsp mustard, or to taste
¼ cup dried bread crumbs

1. Heat oven 200°C. Discard the stems of spinach and wash leaves well under running water. Finely chop the spinach leaves. Pat dry the leaves.
2. Heat butter. Add garlic and green chillies. Stir and add the spinach. Cook

till water evaporates. Sprinkle some salt & pepper. Remove from heat.
3. In a small oven proof dish, spread the cooked spinach.
4. Heat 2 cups of milk in a heavy bottomed sauce pan with a bay leaf and cinnamon stick. Bring the milk to a boil and add the chopped vegetables. Reduce heat and simmer covered till done.
5. Meanwhile dissolve cornflour and maida in the remaining ½ cup of milk.
6. When vegetables get just cooked (do not make them too soft), add the dissolved cornflour and maida to the vegetables. Cook till sauce thickens.
7. Add 4 tbsp grated cheese, butter, salt, pepper and mustard. Remove from heat. Discard the bay leaf and cinnamon stick.
8. Pour the cooked vegetables on the spinach and level with a spoon. Sprinkle bread crumbs. Sprinkle left over cheese. Bake for 8 minutes at 210°C. Serve with buttered toasts or bread buns.

Jhatpat TiP:

- For jhatpat crumbs, microwave white or brown bread slices for 3-4 minutes on high power, mixing once in between to turn sides. Let it stand for 2 minutes to dry out. Grind in a mixer to get jhatpat crumbs.

CAULIFLOWER & COTTAGE CHEESE BAKE

Cooking time : 15 minutes   *Serves 4*

100 gm paneer - cut into ¼" pieces, 1 cauliflower - cut into ½" florets (2 cups)
1 tbsp butter, salt & freshly ground pepper, 50 gm mozerella cheese - grated
2½ tbsp butter, 1 tsp oregano, 3 tbsp maida, 2 cups milk, ½ tsp red chilli flakes
½ tsp mustard, ½ tsp peppercorns - crushted, 3/4 tsp salt, or to taste

1. Heat oven to 200°C.
2. Boil 4-5 cups water with 1 tsp salt & juice of ½ lemon. Add cauliflower. Boil for only 2-3 minutes, keeping it crisp - tender. Strain & wipe dry.
3. Heat butter in a kadhai. Saute cauliflower for 2-3 minutes till brown specs appear. Add some salt and pepper. Transfer to a greased oven proof dish.
4. Sprinkle some salt & coarsely ground peppercorns on paneer. Sprinkle paneer on the cauliflower in the dish.
4. For sauce, heat butter. Add flour. Mix and add oregano. Cook on low heat for 1 minute. Add milk and stir. Add mustard, salt, pepper & red chilli flakes. Stir continuously till the sauce starts coating the back of the spoon.
5. Remove from fire. Add ½ of the grated cheese. Pour sauce over the paneer. Sprinkle chopped parsley or coriander & left over cheese. Bake for 7-8 minutes in a hot oven at 210°C till cheese melts.

SAUCY SPAGHETTI CASSEROLE

Cooking time : 12 minutes

Spaghetti topped with a red tomato based sauce.

Serves 4-5

200 gm spaghetti - boiled (5 cups)
2 tbsp olive oil, 1 tbsp butter
2 spring onions - cut into slices or ½ onion - chopped and ½ capsicum - cut into small thin fingers
salt, freshly ground pepper to taste, 2 tbsp cream or milk
30-50 gm of processed or parmesan cheese - grated

SAUCE

3-4 tbsp olive oil or any cooking oil, 6-7 flakes garlic - crushed
150-200 gm mushrooms - sliced, 1 capsicum - cut into ½" pieces
4 large tomatoes - blended to puree, ¼ cup (4 tbsp) tomato puree
¼ tsp chilli flakes, 1 tsp oregano, ½ tsp sugar, 1 tsp salt, or to taste

TOPPING

75-100 gm paneer - crumbled
100 gm mozzarella cheese - grated

1. Heat oven to 200°C.
2. Heat 7-8 cups of water in a large pan with 2 tsp salt and 2 tsp oil. Holding the bunch of spaghetti in the hand, gradually slide it into the boiling water. Cook uncovered for about 5 minutes or till done. Drain the cooked spaghetti and refresh under cold water.
3. While the spaghetti is boiling, prepare the sauce. Heat oil in a kadhai and add the garlic. Wait for about ½ minute.
4. Stir and add the mushrooms and capsicum. Saute for 1-2 minutes.
5. Add freshly pureed tomatoes. Cook till moisture of the tomatoes evaporates.
6. Add ready made tomato puree, chilli flakes, oregano, sugar, salt and pepper. Add ½ cup of water and bring to boil. Remove from heat.
7. To assemble, heat a clean pan with olive oil and butter. Add spring onions and stir for a few seconds.
8. Add the spaghetti and stir well to coat in butter and oil. Sprinkle salt and freshly ground pepper.
9. Add milk or cream and cheese. Mix and remove to an oven proof dish.
10. Pour the prepared sauce over it.
11. Top with crumbled paneer and grated mozzarella cheese. To serve, grill for 4-5 minutes. Serve hot.

CHINESE STIR FRIED VEGGIES ON RICE

Picture on page 2   *Cooking time : 10 minutes*

Serves 4

1¼ cups rice
1 small carrot - cut into ½" cubes
¼ cup cauliflower or broccoli - cut into small, flat florets
1 small onion - cut into 4 pieces and separated
4-5 mushrooms - cut into slices
4-6 baby corns - cut into half lengthwise (optional)
1 capsicum - cut into ½" cubes
1 tbsp soya sauce, 2½ tbsp tomato sauce, ½ tbsp vinegar
¼ tsp freshly ground pepper, 1 tsp salt, or to taste, a pinch ajinomoto (optional)
3 tbsp cornflour mixed with ¼ cup water
2-3 tbsp oil
2 dried, red chillies - broken into small pieces
8-10 flakes garlic - crushed

1. Boil washed rice in 4-5 cups of salted water. Drain after it gets cooked. Cover and keep aside.
2. While the rice is boiling, cut carrots and capsicum into ½" pieces. Break cauliflower into small florets and cut each floret into two. Slice mushrooms and baby corns. Cut onion into fours and separate the slices. Dissolve cornflour in ¼ cup water and keep aside.
3. Heat oil in a kadhai. Reduce heat and add broken red chillies and garlic.
4. Stir and add baby corns, carrots, cauliflower, onion and mushrooms. Stir for 2-3 minutes. Add capsicum. Add salt & pepper.
5. Stir and add tomato sauce, soya sauce and vinegar. Pour 2 cups of water and bring to a boil. Lower heat and simmer for ½ minute. Add the dissolved cornflour and cook till the vegetables get done and the sauce turns thick.
6. Spread the warm rice in a serving plate. Pour the hot vegetables over the rice and serve immediately.

TiP:

- Add garlic and chillies on low heat as garlic and chillies burn quickly.

PEPPERY AUBERGINES

Cooking time : 12 minutes

Delicious baingans - must give it a try!

Serves 4

1 large (round) baingan (aubergine)
2 tbsp oil
5-6 flakes garlic - crushed
1 onion - cut into 4 pieces and separated
1 green capsicum - deseeded and cut into 1" cubes
1 tomato - deseeded & cubed
2 tbsp tomato sauce
1 tsp soya sauce
1 tsp Worcestershire sauce
½ tsp freshly ground pepper
½ tsp salt, or to taste

1. Wash and chop baingan into 2" cubes. Sprinkle 1 tsp salt and keep aside for 7-8 minutes in a colander (a big strainer with large holes, normally used for straining rice.) This salting is called degorging and removes the bitterness in the aubergines.
2. Meanwhile cut the onion into fours and open the layers of the onion. Cut capsicum into 1" pieces, deseed the tomato and cut into cubes. Keep aside. Peel and crush garlic. Keep aside.
3. Heat oil for frying in a kadhai.
4. Rinse the baingans with water nicely. Pat dry on a kitchen towel. Fry the baingans till brown. They should turn light brown and not remain whitish. Drain on paper napkins.
5. Heat 2 tbsp oil in a kadhai. Add garlic, stir add the onion and the capsicum. Saute for 1 minute.
6. Add the fried aubergines, cubed tomato and all the three sauces.
7. Add ½ tsp salt and freshly crushed peppercorns. Serve hot with garlic bread.

RICE

When you are really hungry, there is nothing more satisfying than a quick hot meal of vegetable or dal pullao with just plain curd or even just by itself.

- The rice should preferably be soaked for 15 minutes before cooking.
- When cooking rice in a pan, add double the quantity of water than that of rice. 1 cup of rice will need 2 cups of water.
- If the rice is to be cooked in a pressure cooker, add equal quantity of water.
- Since in Jhat Pat cooking the rice is not soaked, so add ½ cup of extra water, so 1 cup of uncooked rice will need 2½ cups water when boiled in a pan and 1½ cups when cooked in a pressure cooker.

DAAL BIRYANI

Cooking time : 15 minutes

Serves 2-3

1 cup rice, ½ cup saboot moong dal (green daal)
1 tsp jeera (cumin seeds), 1 onion - cut into slices
2" piece ginger - chopped finely, 2 green chillies - chopped finely
6-8 saboot kali.mirch (peppercorns) - crushed
2 tbsp tomato puree, ½ tsp garam masala, ½ tsp red chilli powder
2 tbsp chopped poodina (mint) or coriander, salt to taste, juice of ½ lemon

1. Soak rice and keep aside. Heat 3 tbsp oil in a pressure cooker. Add jeera.
2. When jeera turns golden, add onions, ginger, green chillies & peppercorns.
3. Stir till onions turn light brown. Reduce heat. Add tomato puree.
4. Cook for 1 minute on low heat. Add washed dal, ½ tsp salt, garam masala, red chilli pd & 2½ cups water. Mix well. Pressure cook to give 1 whistle. Release pressure by putting cooker under running water. Open the lid.
5. Add the rice, coriander or mint, ½ tsp salt and lemon juice. Pressure cook to give 1 whistle. Keep it on low heat for 1 minute. Remove from fire. Keep aside till pressure drops. Serve with tomato-onion raita.

TAHIREE (VEGETABLE MASALA RICE)

Cooking time : 10 minutes

A complete meal with some curd.

Serves 3-4

1 cup rice
2 onions - chopped
3 tomatoes - chopped
2 tbsp ginger-garlic paste
5 tbsp oil
2 cups finely chopped vegetables (potatoes, cauliflower, peas, carrot, beans)
½ tsp chilli powder
1 tsp garam masala
2 tsp salt, or to taste

1. Heat oil in pressure cooker. Add onions and stir fry on medium heat till golden brown.
2. Meanwhile chop the vegetables.
3. When the onions are golden brown add the ginger-garlic paste. Bhuno for 1 minute.
4. Add tomatoes and stir fry for a few seconds.
5. Add the vegetables and bhuno for 1 minute.
6. Wash the rice and add to the vegetables in the cooker. Add salt, chilli powder and garam masala. Bhuno rice for 1 minute.
7. Measure 1½ cups water and add to the cooker.
8. Close the lid and pressure cook to give 1 whistle. Keep on low heat for 1 minute. Remove from heat and keep aside for 5 minutes till the pressure drops.
9. Serve hot rice with plain curd or raita.

SPICY RED MEXICAN RICE

Cooking time : 4 minutes

Serves 4
3 cups boiled rice
3-4 tbsp chopped coriander leaves
2 tbsp oil
1 tsp oregano or 3/4 tsp ajwain (carom seeds)
2 onions - finely chopped
4 tbsp tomato puree
1 tbsp tomato ketchup
1½ tsp salt or to taste, 1 tsp red chilli powder
½ tsp freshly ground saboot kaali mirch (peppercorns)

1. Heat oil in a big kadhai or a wok. Reduce flame. Add oregano or ajwain.
2. After a few seconds, add onions and stir fry till light brown.
3. Add tomato puree. Cook for 1 minute.
4. Reduce flame. Add tomato sauce, red chilli powder, salt and peppercorns.
5. Add the rice. Stir fry gently for 2 minutes.
6. Add chopped coriander. Mix well. Serve hot.

MEALS OUT OF LEFTOVERS

There are days when there are lots of leftovers in the fridge, for example, a bowl of rajma or channas, boiled rice, dal or any vegetable. Here are some innovative ideas which will turn your leftovers into an entirely new tasty Jhatpat meal for your family.

CHANNA BIRYANI

Cooking time : 15 minutes

Serves 2

1½ cups of leftover khatte channe or white or black channas in gravy
3 tbsp oil
1 cup basmati rice
1 onion - chopped
1 tbsp ginger-garlic paste or grate 1" piece ginger and 5-6 flakes garlic
2 tbsp tomato puree
¼ cup poodina (mint leaves) - chopped
2 tsp ready made biryani masala or ½ tsp garam masala
3/4 tsp salt, or to taste

1. Add 1½ cups of water to the cooked channa. Strain and collect the water or gravy in a bowl, (it should measure to 1½ cups.)
2. Wash the rice and keep aside.
3. Heat oil in a pressure cooker. Add onion and stir till light brown.
4. Meanwhile grate the ginger garlic, pluck the mint leaves and wash them.
5. Add ginger-garlic to the onions in the cooker and stir for few seconds.
6. Add the tomato puree, biryani masala and salt.
7. Add the drained channas and mint. Stir.
8. Add the rice and 1½ cups of drained gravy. Pressure cook to one whistle and keep on low heat for 1 minute. Remove from heat.
9. After the pressure drops, serve hot with curd or cucumber raita.

ENCHILADAS WITH WHITE SAUCE

Cooking time : 9 minutes

Serves 2-3

1 cup of cooked leftover rajma curry
1 tbsp tomato puree, ½ tbsp hot tomato sauce
4 thin chappaties
4 tbsp chopped capsicum
4 tbsp chopped tomato
4 tbsp chopped spring onions or lettuce

SAUCE

1¼ tbsp maida
1 tbsp butter
1½ cups milk
2-3 tbsp chopped green coriander
¼ tsp salt & ¼ tsp pepper, or to taste
100 gm mozzarella or pizza cheese

Quick Tiramisu : recipe on page 99 ➢

1. Mash the rajma with a potato masher to a rough paste. Heat the mashed rajma and tomato puree in a kadhai and cook till the liquid dries up and the rajma turns thick. Add tomato sauce. Remove from heat.
2. Heat oven 200°C.
3. To prepare the sauce, heat butter in a clean kadhai. Add maida and stir for 1 minute. Add milk and stir continuously till the sauce starts to coat the spoon. Add coriander, salt and pepper to taste. Remove from heat.
4. To assemble, take a thin soft chappati and spread some rajma on half the chappati.
5. Top with 1 tbsp each of chopped capsicum, tomato and spring onions.
6. Roll the chappati tightly and place the chappati in an ovenproof plate dish with the joint side down. Lay all the chappati rolls side by side.
7. Pour sauce to cover the chappaties completely.
8. Top with grated cheese. Sprinkle some spring onion greens or capsicum.
9. Grill in hot oven for 2-3 minutes till cheese melts.

TiP:

- After using the milk in the morning, try kneading the dough for chappaties in the milk waala vessel. You will get really soft chappaties.

AJWAINI DAAL PARANTHA

Cooking time : 5 minutes

Serves 2-3

1 cup leftover cooked dal
1¼ - 1½ cups atta (wheat flour)
½ tsp ajwain (carom seeds), ½ tsp garam masala, salt to taste
1 green chilli - chopped finely, 2 tbsp green coriander - chopped

1. Mix all the ingredients in a paraat. Knead to a soft dough without using any water, so add just enough atta to get a proper dough.
2. Roll out a thick chappati and smear little ghee. Fold into half and again into half to get a triangle. Roll out to get a triangular parantha.
3. Heat a tawa and cook parantha on both sides. Add a little ghee on one side and overturn. Press the top and sides of the parantha with a large spoon or karchhi to get a crisp parantha. Serve with curd.

TiP:

- You may add 20-25 thinly shredded leaves of paalak (spinach) to get a more nutritive and a more delicious parantha.

LEMON RICE

Cooking time : 5 minutes

Serves 4
3 cups boiled rice
juice of 2 lemons
¼ tsp haldi (turmeric powder)
1 tsp sugar
1½ tsp salt or to taste

TEMPERING (CHHOWNK)
2 tbsp oil
1 tsp sarson (mustard seeds)
1 tbsp channe ki dal (split gram dal)
3 dry, red chillies - broken into pieces
few curry leaves

1. Spread the boiled rice on a tray under a fan for the grains to separate.
2. Mix lemon juice, haldi, salt and sugar together in a small bowl.
3. Heat oil in kadhai. Reduce flame. Add sarson, dal & red chillies. Cook on very low flame till dal just starts changing colour. Do not let the dal turn brown.
4. Add curry leaves.
5. Add the lemon juice mixture. Add ¼ cup water.
6. Cover and simmer on low flame till dal turns soft and the water dries. Check the dal carefully to see that it is no longer too crunchy.
7. Add rice and stir gently till well mixed for 2-3 minutes. Serve hot.

DESSERTS

Unexpected guests! There is no reason why you cannot prepare a dessert, even if the time is limited. You will find many imaginative ideas in the following chapters for delightful desserts, but remember to follow the instructions carefully to get a perfect dessert in a jiffy. I would recommend that you try these when you have enough time so that you can prepare them confidently even when you are hard pressed for time.

QUICK TRIFLE

Cooking time : 4 minutes

Serves 8

3-4 black forest pastries or any other pastries
1 tin mixed tinned fruit or 2 cups chopped fresh fruits
1 family pack (500 ml) vanilla ice cream
1-2 tbsp chocolate sauce to top
a few almonds - cut into thin long pieces

1. Cut the pastries into 3 slices. (Open the layers of the pastry). Place them in a shallow serving dish covering the bottom of the dish.
2. Take a knife and spread the cream of the top layer evenly on the pastries.
3. Soak the pastries with 4-5 tbsp of the mixed fruit syrup (should feel slightly moist). If using fresh fruit, soak the pastries with cold milk.
4. Spread the drained, canned fruit or chopped fresh fruit on the pastries.
5. At serving time, top the fruit with scoops of ice cream.
6. Pour a few swirls of chocolate sauce on the ice cream.
7. Decorate with some almonds and serve.

BREAD PUDDING

Preparation time : 5 minutes

A hot winter pudding. The pudding takes just 5 minutes to get ready, although the baking time is quite a lot. I still find it jhatpat because you can put it in the oven while the dinner is going on and serve it hot straight from the oven.

Serves 4

4 slices whole wheat bread - buttered
2-3 tbsp desiccated coconut (coconut powder)
10-12 almonds - chopped
15-20 raisins - halved
2 cups milk
3 tbsp cornflour
¼ cup sugar
1 tsp vanilla essence

TOPPING

2 tsp butter to dot
1 tbsp brown sugar
a pinch of nutmeg (jaiphal) powder

1. Cut sides of bread and cut into 1" cubes. Grease a small dish, arrange half of the bread pieces to cover the bottom.
2. Sprinkle 1 tbsp of coconut on the bread.
3. Sprinkle 1/3 of the nuts.
4. Arrange a second layer of bread and sprinkle coconut and nuts. Keep aside.
5. Dissolve cornflour in ½ cup of milk. Heat the rest (1½ cups) of milk with sugar and boil. Add cornflour paste and cook stirring till thick.
6. Remove from fire and add 1 tsp vanilla essence to the custard.
7. Pour the hot custard over the bread.
8. Top with brown sugar and sprinkle nuts. Dot with butter.
9. Bake for 30 minutes at 200°C. Remove from oven and sprinkle nutmeg powder. Serve hot during winters.

CREAMY LEMON DESSERT

Picture on facing page   *Cooking time : 15 minutes*

Serves 4-5

250 gm (1¼ cups) fresh cream
½ tin (3/4 cup) condensed milk - cold
¼ cup lemon juice (juice of 4 lemons)
rind (peel) of 1 lemon, a pinch or a few drops yellow colour

CRUST
1 packet (10) good day biscuits
4 tbsp (50 gm) melted butter

1. Keep the cream in a bowl and chill for 10 minutes in the freezer.
2. To prepare the crust, preheat oven to 180°C. Break good day biscuits into pieces and put in a polythene. Crush to a coarse powder with a belan (rolling pin). Do not make them too fine. Put them in a bowl.
3. Melt butter and add 4 tbsp melted butter to the biscuit crumbs. Mix well.
4. Spread crumbs in the serving dish, (a small square borosil dish in fine). Press well. Bake at 180°C for 10 minutes. Remove from oven and cool.

5. While the crust is being baked, wash & grate 1 lemon with the peel gently on the grater to get lemon rind. Do not apply pressure and see that the white pith beneath the lemon peel is not grated along with the yellow rind.
6. Take out ¼ cup lemon juice. Add the rind to it.
7. Empty ½ tin of cold condensed milk (keep condensed milk in fridge) into a bowl. Add lemon juice and beat well. The condensed milk turns thick on whipping. Keep in the fridge.
8. Beat chilled cream in the chilled bowl with an electric egg beater (hand mixer) till soft peaks are formed. After **soft** peaks are ready, beat gently with a **spoon** till **firm** peaks are formed. Beat carefully in a cool place or over ice, taking care not to beat vigorously. The cream should remain smooth and not turn buttery or granular. Put about ½ cup cream in an icing bag for decoration and keep in the fridge.
9. Add half of the thickened condensed milk to the cream in the bowl. Fold condensed milk gently into the cream to mix well. Fold in the left over condensed milk too. Add enough colour to get a nice yellow colour.
10. Pour the cream mix over the cooled biscuit crust in the dish. Keep in the fridge for atleast 3 hours to chill and if you want to serve soon, chill in the freezer compartment for ½ to 1 hour. To serve, cut into squares.

QUICK TIRAMISU

Cooking time : 17 minutes *Picture on page 86*

The dessert takes very little time to get ready, although the setting time in the refrigerator is at least an hour. I still find it jhatpat because you can chill it in the freezer while the dinner is going on and serve it straight from there.

Serves 5-6

400 gm (2 cups) fresh cream - chilled
1 tsp vanilla essence
½ cup powder sugar
1 tbsp rum or brandy (optional)
2-3 tbsp cocoa to sprinkle

ESPRESSO COFFEE (½ CUP)

¼ cup water, ½ cup milk
1 tsp coffee, 2 tsp sugar

SPONGE FINGERS

2 eggs
5 tbsp powdered sugar, 5 tbsp maida (plain flour)
1 tsp baking powder, 1 tsp vanilla essence

1. Chill cream in a beating bowl in the freezer for 10 minutes. Chill the blades of the beater or the wire whisk also.
2. Preheat the oven to 180°C. Prepare the sponge fingers in the meanwhile. Beat eggs till frothy and double in volume. Add sugar and beat some more. Sift maida with baking powder and add to the eggs. Gently fold in the maida. Add the essence also. Pour in a greased loaf tin or a rectangular tray (9" long and 4" wide). Bake in a preheated oven at 180°C for 12 minutes till it shrinks away from the sides. Remove from tray. Keep aside to cool. (If you wish, make an eggless cake and cut into fingers or buy a ready made sponge cake from any bakery
3. Meanwhile, whip the cream with sugar, essence and brandy till **soft peaks** form. Beat cream over ice or in a cool room during the hot weather. Now gently beat some more with a **tablespoon** till **firm peaks** are formed. Do not over beat. If the cream starts looking granular, immediately stop beating. Put whipped cream in the freezer for a few minutes.
4. To prepare espresso coffee boil water and milk together. Simmer for a minute. Add sugar. Mix. Remove from fire. Add coffee and mix well. Cool to room temperature.

5. Cut sponge fingers into two lengthways. Arrange sponge fingers with cut side up at the bottom of a small rectangular borosil dish. Sprinkle half of the prepared espresso coffee on the sponge to soak.
6. Spread ½ of the whipped cream. Level it gently.
7. Again put a layer of sponge cake and soak with coffee as above.
8. Spread the remaining cream and level gently. Chill in the freezer for 10 minutes.
9. Sift 2 tbsp cocoa through a strainer over the dessert. Decorate with fresh cherries and mint. Cover with a cling film and keep to chill for atleast 1-2 hours till well set. Cut into squares to serve.

Jhatpat TiP : You may buy ready made sponge cake and cut into thin fingers.

APPLE CRUMBLE

Cooking time : 12 minutes

Serves 4-6
5-6 apples
1 tsp lemon juice
½ tsp dalchini (cinnamon) powder
4-5 tbsp sugar
8-10 glucose biscuits
2 tsp cold butter (yellow or white)
¼ cup walnuts or 12-15 almonds - chopped

1. Peel and cut the apples into small pieces.
2. Place the chopped apples in a pan. Add sugar, lemon juice and cinnamon powder and cook till water evaporates (try not to mash the apples). Remove from fire.
3. Mix walnuts or almonds to the apples and transfer to an oven proof dish.
4. Roughly crush the biscuits and mix the cold butter with the biscuits.
5. Spread biscuits over the apples. Bake in a preheated oven at 200°C for 6 minutes. Serve hot or cold with sweetened thin cream or vanilla ice cream.

KESARI SEVIYAAN

Cooking time : 11 minutes

Serves 3-4

1 cup bambino's seviyaan (vermicelli)
2 tbsp ghee, 3-4 tbsp sugar
8-10 kismish, a few almonds - chopped, a few pistas - chopped
seeds of 2 chhoti illaichi (green cardamoms) - crushed
few strands kesar (saffron) - dissolved in ¼ cup warm milk, pinch orange colour

1. Heat ghee in a heavy bottomed kadhai. Add vermicelli and stir on medium heat for 3-4 minutes or till dark golden brown, but do not burn them.
2. Add 1 cup of water and bring to a boil. Lower heat and cover the kadhai. Cook till the seviyaan are soft and the water is absorbed. Check seviyaan, they should be really soft or they will harden when you add sugar.)
3. Add the kesar milk, cardamom seeds, kismish, almonds and a pinch of colour. Cook till dry.
4. Add the sugar and cook for 1-2 minutes on low heat.
5. Remove from heat and keep aside for 1-2 minutes for the seviyaan to absorb the sugar well. Serve hot garnished with pistas and almonds.

Nita Mehta's BEST SELLERS (Vegetarian)

INDIAN Vegetarian

NEW CHINESE

NEW MICROWAVE

Eggless Desserts

Indian **LOW FAT**

Vegetarian **CURRIES**

QUICK MEALS

More **PANEER**

Dal & Roti

Desserts Puddings

MUGHLAI
Vegetarian Khaana

Green Vegetables